the farmer's market
cookbook

the farmer's market
cookbook

recipes for fabulous farmhouse food

emma summer

HERMES HOUSE

This edition is published by Hermes House, an imprint of Anness Publishing Ltd, Hermes House,
88–89 Blackfriars Road, London SE1 8HA; tel. 020 7401 2077; fax 020 7633 9499

www.hermeshouse.com; www.annesspublishing.com

If you like the images in this book and would like to investigate using them for publishing, promotions or advertising,
please visit our website www.practicalpictures.com for more information.

Publisher: Joanna Lorenz
Project Editors: Gaby Goldsack, Lucy Pery
Editor: Jenni Fleetwood
Recipe contributors: Carla Capalbo, Jacqueline Clark, Maxine Clark Cleary, Carole Clements, Stephanie Donaldson,
Joanna Farrow, Christine France, Christine Ingram, Judy Jackson, Patricia Lousada, Norma MacMillan, Katherine Richmond,
Laura Washburn, Steven Wheeler, Elizabeth Wolf-Cohen
Photographers: Karl Adamson, Edward Allwright, James Duncan, John Freeman, Michelle Garrett, Amanda Heywood,
Patrick McLeavey
Illustrator: Anna Koska
Designer: Siân Keogh, Axis Design
Production Controller: Mai-Ling Collyer

ETHICAL TRADING POLICY
Because of our ongoing ecological investment programme, you, as our customer, can have the pleasure and reassurance of knowing
that a tree is being cultivated on your behalf to naturally replace the materials used to make the book you are holding. For further
information about this scheme, go to www.annesspublishing.com/trees

A CIP catalogue record for this book is available from the British Library.

Previously published as part of a larger volume, *The Farmhouse Cookbook*

NOTES
For all recipes, quantities are given in both metric and imperial measures and, where appropriate, in standard cups and spoons.
Follow one set of measures, but not a mixture, because they are not interchangeable.
Standard spoon and cup measures are level. 1 tsp = 5ml, 1 tbsp = 15ml, 1 cup = 250ml/8fl oz.
Australian standard tablespoons are 20ml. Australian readers should use 3 tsp in place of 1 tbsp for measuring small quantities.
American pints are 16fl oz/2 cups. American readers should use 20fl oz/2.5 cups in place of 1 pint when measuring liquids.
Electric oven temperatures in this book are for conventional ovens. When using a fan oven, the temperature will probably need to be
reduced by about 10–20°C/20–40°F. Since ovens vary, you should check with your manufacturer's instruction book for guidance.
Medium (US large) eggs are used unless otherwise stated.

Contents

———————

———————

Introduction

Country cooking evokes the picture of an idyllic farmhouse setting, located in the depths of the luscious green countryside. However, the true essence of country cuisine is less a matter of geography than about using good quality, natural and seasonally fresh ingredients to create simple but flavourful food throughout the year.

The best home cooking could be defined by the adage "less is more". If you are preparing fresh game or fish, why would you want to disguise their own unique flavours with complicated sauces? The real skill is in the way that you can enhance food naturally as you cook it, using herbs and traditional cooking styles to bring out the rich flavours of all kinds of meats, fish, vegetables, fruits and dairy produce.

With the superb variety of organic ingredients that are now available, it has never been easier, or more enjoyable, to create food that makes full use of the riches of the countryside.

This recipe collection takes its inspiration from the wealth of traditional country kitchen dishes from all over the world. It includes soups, pies, casseroles, stews, desserts, bakes, pickles and preserves – to bring the wholesome taste of the country to your table.

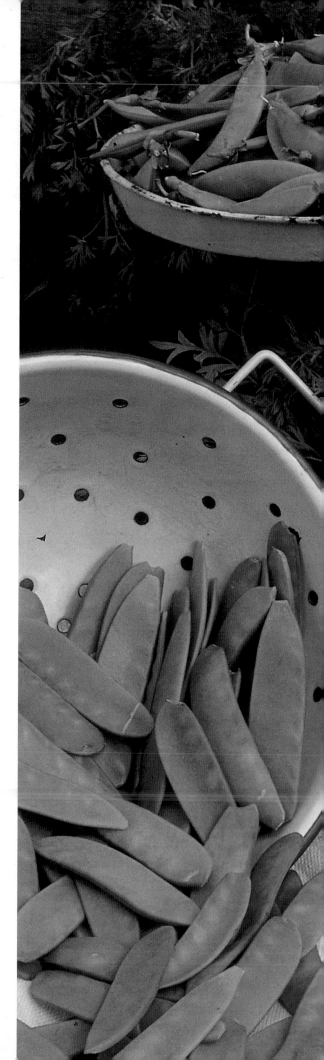

SOUPS AND STARTERS

Pear and Watercress Soup with Stilton Croûtons

*Pears and Stilton taste very good when you eat them together after the main course —
here, for a change, they are served as a starter.*

INGREDIENTS

1 bunch watercress
4 medium pears, sliced
900 ml/1½ pints chicken stock,
preferably home-made
salt and pepper
120 ml/4 fl oz double cream
juice of 1 lime

For the croûtons
25 g/1 oz butter
30 ml/1 tbsp olive oil
200 g/7 oz cubed stale bread
140 g/5 oz chopped Stilton cheese

Serves 6

1

Keep back about a third of the watercress leaves. Place all the rest of the watercress leaves and stalks in a pan with the pears, stock and a little seasoning. Simmer for about 15–20 minutes.

2

Reserving some watercress leaves for garnishing, add the rest of the leaves and immediately blend in a food processor until smooth.

3

Put the mixture into a bowl and stir in the cream and lime juice to mix the flavours thoroughly. Season again to taste. Pour all the soup back into a pan and reheat, stirring gently until warmed through.

4

To make the croûtons, melt the butter and oil and fry the bread cubes until golden brown. Drain on kitchen paper. Put the cheese on top and heat under a hot grill until bubbling. Reheat the soup and pour into bowls. Divide the croûtons and remaining watercress between the bowls.

Green Bean Soup with Parmesan

Make the most of a garden glut of green beans by serving this colourful summer soup.

INGREDIENTS

25 g / 1 oz / 2 tbsp butter
225 g / 8 oz green beans, trimmed
1 garlic clove, crushed
475 ml / 16 fl oz / 2 cups vegetable
stock
50 g / 2 oz / ⅔ cup Parmesan cheese
60 ml / 4 tbsp single cream
30 ml / 2 tbsp chopped fresh parsley
salt and freshly ground black pepper

Serves 4

1

Melt the butter in a saucepan and cook the green beans and garlic for 2–3 minutes over a medium heat, stirring frequently. Stir in the stock with salt and pepper to taste. Bring to the boil. Reduce the heat and simmer for 10–15 minutes, until the beans are tender.

2

Process the soup until smooth. Alternatively, purée the soup in a food mill. Return it to the clean pan and heat gently. Stir in the Parmesan and cream. Sprinkle with the parsley and serve.

Lentil and Vegetable Soup

Unlike red lentils, the brown variety retain their shape after cooking and add texture to this hearty country soup.

INGREDIENTS

175 g / 6 oz / 1 cup brown lentils
1 litre / 1¾ pints / 4 cups chicken
stock
250 ml / 8 fl oz / 1 cup water
60 ml / 4 tbsp dry red wine
675 g / 1½ lb tomatoes, skinned,
seeded and chopped, or 400 g / 14 oz
canned chopped tomatoes
1 carrot, sliced
1 onion, chopped
1 celery stick, sliced
1 garlic clove, crushed
¼ tsp ground coriander
10 ml / 2 tsp snipped fresh basil, or
½ tsp dried basil
1 bay leaf
90 ml / 6 tbsp freshly grated
Parmesan cheese

Serves 6

1

Put the lentils in a sieve. Rinse under cold running water, then discard any discoloured ones and any grit.

2

Put the lentils in a large saucepan. Add all the remaining ingredients, except the Parmesan, and bring to the boil.

3

Reduce the heat to low, cover and simmer for 20–25 minutes, stirring occasionally. When the lentils are tender, discard the bay leaf and ladle the soup into 6 warmed bowls. Sprinkle each portion with 15 ml / 1 tbsp of the Parmesan.

NOTE
For a more substantial soup, add about 115 g / 4 oz / ½ cup finely chopped cooked ham for the last 10 minutes of cooking.

Barley Soup

A feature of the farmhouse kitchen is the stockpot simmering on the stove. With a good home-made stock on hand, it only takes a few simple ingredients to make an excellent soup.

INGREDIENTS

900 g / 2 lb meaty bones (lamb, beef
or veal)
900 ml / 1½ pints / 3¾ cups water
30 ml / 2 tbsp oil
3 carrots, finely chopped
4 celery sticks, finely sliced
1 onion, finely chopped
30 ml / 2 tbsp pearl barley
salt and freshly ground black pepper

Serves 4

NOTE
All soups taste better with home-made stock. The long slow simmering can be done well in advance and stocks freeze well. A quick version of this soup can be made using water and a stock cube, but it won't have the same flavour.

1
Preheat the oven to 200°C / 400°F / Gas Mark 6. To prepare the meat stock, brown the lamb, beef or veal bones in a roasting tin in the oven for about 30 minutes. Put the bones in a large saucepan, cover with the water and bring to the boil.

2
Use a metal spoon to skim off the surface froth, then cover the pan and simmer the stock for at least 2 hours. Heat the oil in a saucepan and sauté the carrots, celery and onion for about 1 minute. Strain the stock into the pan.

3
Add the barley to the pan of vegetables and continue cooking for about 1 hour, until the barley is soft. Season the soup with plenty of salt and pepper, transfer to serving bowls and serve hot.

Bacon and Lentil Soup

Serve this hearty soup with chunks of warm, crusty bread.

INGREDIENTS

*450 g/1 lb thick-sliced
bacon, cubed
1 onion, roughly chopped
1 small turnip, roughly chopped
1 celery stick, chopped
1 carrot, sliced
1 potato, peeled and
roughly chopped
75 g/3 oz/½ cup lentils
1 bouquet garni
freshly ground black pepper*

Serves 4

1

Heat a large pan and add the bacon. Cook for
a few minutes, allowing the fat to run out.

2

Add all the vegetables and cook for
4 minutes.

3

Add the lentils, bouquet garni, seasoning
and enough water to cover. Bring to the boil
and simmer for 1 hour, or until the lentils
are tender.

Mushroom Picker's Pâté

One of the delights of country living is to rise early and go on a mushrooming expedition with an expert who knows precisely what to pick. The pâté is the perfect reward.

INGREDIENTS

45 ml / 3 tbsp vegetable oil
1 onion, chopped
½ celery stick, chopped
350 g / 12 oz mushrooms, sliced
150 g / 5 oz / ⅔ cup red lentils
475 ml / 16 fl oz / 2 cups water or
vegetable stock
1 fresh thyme sprig

50 g / 2 oz / 4 tbsp almond nut butter
1 garlic clove, crushed
1 thick slice white bread, crusts removed
75 ml / 5 tbsp milk
15 ml / 1 tbsp lemon juice
4 egg yolks
celery salt and ground black pepper

Serves 6

1

Preheat the oven to 180°C / 350°F / Gas Mark 4. Brown the onion and celery in the oil. Add the mushrooms and soften for 3–4 minutes. Remove a spoonful of the mushroom pieces and set it aside.

2

Add the lentils, water or stock and thyme to the mushroom mixture. Bring to the boil, then lower the heat and simmer for 20 minutes or until the lentils are very soft.

3

Place the nut butter, garlic, bread and milk in a food processor and process until smooth.

4

Add the lemon juice and egg yolks and process briefly. Tip in the lentil mixture, process until smooth, then season with the celery salt and pepper. Lastly, stir the reserved mushrooms into the mixture.

5

Spoon the mixture into a 1.2 litre / 2 pint / 5 cup pâté dish and cover with foil. Stand the dish in a roasting tin and pour in boiling water to come halfway up the sides of the dish. Cook the pâté for 50 minutes. Allow to cool before serving.

NOTE

If you are using only cultivated mushrooms, an addition of 10 g / ⅓ oz / 3 tbsp of dried porcini will boost the flavour. Soak the dried mushrooms in warm water for 20 minutes before draining and adding to the pan with the fresh mushrooms.

Cheese and Potato Patties

Serve these delicious little potato cakes with a simple tomato salad for an inexpensive but imaginative starter.

INGREDIENTS

500 g / 1¼ lb potatoes
115 g / 4 oz feta or Roquefort cheese
4 spring onions, finely chopped
45 ml / 3 tbsp chopped fresh dill
1 egg, beaten
15 ml / 1 tbsp lemon juice
plain flour, for dredging
45 ml / 3 tbsp olive oil
salt and freshly ground black pepper

Serves 4

TIP
Add salt sparingly when making the potato cakes, as the cheese will be salty.

1

Boil the potatoes in their skins in a saucepan of lightly salted water until soft. Drain, peel and mash while still warm. Crumble the feta cheese or Roquefort into the potatoes and add the spring onions, dill, egg and lemon juice. Season with salt and pepper. Stir well.

2

Cover the mixture and chill until firm. Divide the mixture into walnut-sized balls, then flatten them slightly. Dredge with flour. Heat the oil in a frying pan and fry the potato patties until golden brown on each side. Drain on kitchen paper and serve at once.

Fonduta

Fontina is an Italian medium-fat cheese with a rich salty flavour, a little like Gruyère, which makes a good substitute. This delicious hot dip makes a good starter before a fairly light main course. Serve it with warm crusty bread.

INGREDIENTS

*250 g / 9 oz fontina or Gruyère
cheese, diced
250 ml / 8 fl oz / 1 cup milk
15 g / ½ oz / 1 tbsp butter
2 eggs, lightly beaten
freshly ground black pepper*

Serves 4

NOTE
Do not overheat the sauce, or the eggs may curdle. A very gentle heat will produce a lovely smooth sauce.

1

Put the cheese in a bowl with the milk and leave to soak for 2–3 hours. Transfer to a double boiler or a heatproof bowl set over a pan of simmering water.

2

Add the butter and eggs and stir gently until the cheese has melted to a smooth sauce. Remove from the heat, season with pepper and serve in a warmed serving dish.

VEGETABLE DISHES

Stuffed Tomatoes, with Wild Rice, Corn and Coriander

These tomatoes could be served as a light meal or as an accompaniment for meat or fish.

INGREDIENTS

8 medium tomatoes
50 g/2 oz sweetcorn kernels
2 tbsp white wine
50 g/2 oz cooked wild rice
1 clove garlic
50 g/2 oz grated Cheddar cheese
1 tbsp chopped fresh coriander
salt and pepper
1 tbsp olive oil

Serves 4

1

Cut the tops off the tomatoes and remove the seeds with a small teaspoon. Scoop out all the flesh and chop finely – remember to chop the tops as well.

2

Preheat the oven to 180°C/350°F/Gas Mark 4. Put the chopped tomato in a pan. Add the sweetcorn and the white wine. Cover with a close-fitting lid and simmer until tender. Drain the excess liquid.

3

Mix together all the remaining ingredients except the olive oil, adding salt and pepper to taste. Carefully spoon the mixture into the tomatoes, piling it higher in the centre. Sprinkle the oil over the top, arrange the tomatoes in an ovenproof dish and bake at 180°C/350°F/Gas Mark 4 for about 15–20 minutes, until cooked through.

Peas with Lettuce and Onion

Podding peas is a traditional pastime in the farmhouse kitchen. Sweet young peas taste delicious when cooked with strips of lettuce.

INGREDIENTS

15 g / ½ oz / 1 tbsp butter
1 small onion, finely chopped
1 small round lettuce, halved and
sliced into thin strips
450 g / 1 lb / 3½ cups shelled fresh
peas (from about 1.5 kg / 3½ lb pods),
or thawed frozen peas
45 ml / 3 tbsp water
salt and freshly ground black pepper

Serves 4–6

1

Melt the butter in a heavy-based saucepan. Add the onion and cook over a medium-low heat for about 3 minutes until just softened. Place the lettuce strips on top of the onion and add the peas and water. Season lightly with salt and pepper.

2

Cover the pan tightly and cook the lettuce and peas over a low heat until the peas are tender – fresh peas will take 10–20 minutes, frozen peas about 10 minutes. Toss lightly and serve at once.

Broad Beans with Cream

Skinned broad beans are a beautiful bright green. Try this simple way of serving them.

INGREDIENTS

450 g/1 lb shelled broad beans (from
about 2 kg / 4½ lb pods)
90 ml / 6 tbsp crème fraîche or
whipping cream
salt and freshly ground black pepper
finely snipped chives, to garnish

Serves 4–6

1

Bring a large pan of lightly salted water to the boil and add the beans. Reduce the heat slightly and cook the beans for about 8 minutes until just tender. Drain, refresh under cold running water, then drain again.

2

Remove the skins by slitting each bean and gently squeezing out the kernel.

NOTE
If you can find them, fresh flageolet or lima beans can be served in the same way.

3

Put the skinned beans in a saucepan with the cream and seasoning, cover and heat through gently. Sprinkle with the snipped chives and serve at once.

Roasted Pepper Medley

When roasted, red peppers acquire a marvellous smoky flavour that is wonderful with sun-dried tomatoes and artichoke hearts.

INGREDIENTS

50 g / 2 oz / ½ cup drained sun-dried
tomatoes in oil
3 red peppers
2 yellow or orange peppers
2 green peppers
30 ml / 2 tbsp balsamic vinegar
a few drops of chilli sauce

75 ml / 5 tbsp olive oil
4 drained, canned artichoke hearts,
sliced
1 garlic clove, thinly sliced
salt and freshly ground black pepper
fresh basil leaves, to garnish

Serves 6

1

Preheat the oven to 200°C / 400°F / Gas Mark 6. Slice the sun-dried tomatoes into thin strips. Set aside. Put the whole peppers on an oiled baking sheet and bake for about 45 minutes until beginning to char. Cover with a dish towel and leave to cool for 5 minutes.

2

Mix the vinegar and chilli sauce in a bowl. Whisk in the oil, then season with a little salt and pepper.

3

Peel and slice the peppers. Mix with the artichokes, tomatoes and garlic in a bowl. Toss with the dressing and scatter with the basil leaves.

Baby Aubergines with Raisins and Pine Nuts

Make this simple starter a day in advance, to allow the sour and sweet flavours to develop.

INGREDIENTS

250 ml / 8 fl oz / 1 cup extra virgin olive oil
juice of 1 lemon
30 ml / 2 tbsp balsamic vinegar
3 cloves
25 g / 1 oz / ⅓ cup pine nuts
25 g / 1 oz / 3 tbsp raisins
15 ml / 1 tbsp granulated sugar
1 bay leaf
large pinch of dried chilli flakes
12 baby aubergines, halved lengthways
salt and freshly ground black pepper

Serves 4

TIP
Use sliced aubergines if baby ones are not obtainable, or try this with grilled peppers.

1

Put 175 ml / 6 fl oz / ¾ cup of the olive oil in a jug. Add the lemon juice, vinegar, cloves, pine nuts, raisins, sugar and bay leaf. Stir in the chilli flakes and salt and pepper. Mix well. Preheat the grill.

2

Brush the aubergines with the remaining oil. Grill for 10 minutes, until slightly blackened, turning them over halfway through. Place the hot aubergines in a bowl, and pour over the marinade. Leave to cool, turning the aubergines once or twice. Serve cold.

Stewed Artichokes

*There are lots of wonderful ways to serve artichokes. Try them lightly
stewed with garlic, parsley and wine.*

INGREDIENTS

*1 lemon
4 large or 6 small globe artichokes
25 g / 1 oz / 2 tbsp butter
60 ml / 4 tbsp olive oil
2 garlic cloves, finely chopped
60 ml / 4 tbsp chopped fresh parsley
45 ml / 3 tbsp water
90 ml / 6 tbsp milk
90 ml / 6 tbsp white wine
salt and freshly ground black pepper*

Serves 6

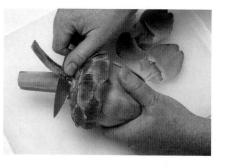

———— 1 ————

Squeeze the lemon juice into a large bowl of
cold water. Put a large pan of water on the
stove and bring to the boil while you
prepare the artichokes one at a time.

———— 2 ————

Cut off the tip from the artichoke's stem.
Peel the stem, pulling off the small leaves
around it, and continue until you reach the
taller inner leaves. Slice off the topmost part
of the leaves. Cut the artichoke into
segments, then cut out the choke from each
segment. Place the artichokes in the
acidulated water, then blanch in the boiling
water for 4–5 minutes. Drain well.

———— 3 ————

Heat the butter and olive oil in a large
saucepan and fry the garlic and parsley for
2–3 minutes. Stir in the artichokes, water
and milk, season, then cook for 10 minutes,
or until the liquid has evaporated. Stir in
the wine, cover and cook until the
artichokes are tender. Serve hot or at
room temperature.

Green Beans with Tomatoes

Green beans in a rich tomato sauce make a dish that is as colourful as it is good to eat.

INGREDIENTS

*45 ml / 3 tbsp olive oil
1 onion, preferably red, very finely
sliced
350 g / 12 oz plum tomatoes, peeled
and finely chopped
120 ml / 4 fl oz / ½ cup water
5–6 fresh basil leaves, torn into shreds
450 g / 1 lb fresh green beans,
trimmed
salt and freshly ground black pepper*

Serves 4–6

———— 1 ————

Heat the oil in a large frying pan. Add the
onion slices and cook for 5–6 minutes,
until just soft. Add the tomatoes and cook
over a medium heat for 6–8 minutes, until
they soften. Stir in the water. Season with
salt and pepper, and add the basil.

———— 2 ————

Stir in the beans, turning them in the pan
to coat them with the sauce. Cover the pan,
and cook over a medium heat for 15–20
minutes, until tender. Stir occasionally, and
add a little more water if the sauce dries
out too much. Serve hot or cold.

FISH AND SEAFOOD

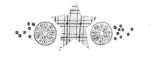

Fish Stew with Calvados, Parsley and Dill

This rustic stew harbours all sorts of interesting flavours and will please and intrigue.
Many varieties of fish can be used, just choose the freshest and best.

INGREDIENTS

1 kg/2 lb assorted white fish
1 tbsp chopped parsley, plus a few
leaves to garnish
225 g/8 oz mushrooms
225 g/8 oz can of tomatoes
salt and pepper
2 tsp flour
15 g/¹⁄₂ oz/1 tbsp butter
450 ml/³⁄₄ pint cider
45 ml/ 3 tbsp Calvados
1 large bunch fresh dill sprigs,
reserving 4 fronds to garnish

Serves 4

1

Chop the fish roughly and place it in a casserole or stewing pot with the parsley, mushrooms and tomatoes, adding salt and pepper to taste.

2

Preheat the oven to 180°C/350°F/Gas Mark 4. Work the flour into the butter. Heat the cider and stir in the flour and butter mixture a little at a time. Cook, stirring, until it has thickened slightly.

3

Add the cider mixture and the remaining ingredients to the fish and mix gently. Cover and bake for about 30 minutes. Serve garnished with sprigs of dill and parsley leaves.

Griddled Trout with Bacon

This dish can also be cooked on the barbecue.

INGREDIENTS

25g / 1oz / 1 tbsp plain flour
4 trout, cleaned and gutted
75g / 3oz streaky bacon
50g / 2oz / 4 tbsp butter
15ml / 1 tbsp olive oil
juice of ½ lemon
salt and freshly ground
black pepper

Serves 4

1

Pat the trout dry with kitchen roll and mix the flour and seasoning together.

2

Roll the trout in the seasoned flour mixture and wrap tightly in the streaky bacon. Heat a heavy frying pan. Heat the butter and oil in the pan and fry the trout for 5 minutes on each side. Serve immediately, with the lemon juice drizzled on top.

Trout Fillets with Spinach and Mushroom Sauce

Field mushrooms form the basis of this rich sauce, served with trout that has been filleted to make it easier to eat.

INGREDIENTS

4 brown or rainbow trout, filleted and skinned to make 8 fillets

For the spinach and mushroom sauce
75 g / 3 oz / 6 tbsp butter
¼ medium onion, chopped
225 g / 8 oz closed field mushrooms, chopped
300 ml / ½ pint / 1¼ cups boiling chicken stock
225 g / 8 oz frozen chopped spinach
10 ml / 2 tsp cornflour, mixed to a paste with 15 ml / 1 tbsp cold water
150 ml / ¼ pint / ⅔ cup crème fraîche grated nutmeg
salt and freshly ground black pepper

Serves 4

NOTE
Spinach and mushroom sauce is also good with fillets of cod, haddock and sole.

2

Stir the cornflour paste into the mushroom mixture. Bring to the boil, then simmer gently to thicken. Purée the mixture. Add the crème fraîche and season with salt, pepper and nutmeg. Blend briefly, then scrape into a serving jug and keep warm.

3

Melt the remaining butter in a large non-stick frying pan. Season the trout and cook for 6 minutes, turning once. Serve with the sauce either poured over or served separately. New potatoes and baby corn would be ideal accompaniments.

1

To make the sauce, melt two-thirds of the butter in a frying pan and fry the onion until soft. Add the mushrooms and cook until the juices begin to run. Stir in the stock and the spinach and cook until the spinach has thawed completely.

Special Seafood Stew

Not all farmhouse cooking is plain and pastoral – on high days and holidays family and friends will celebrate with a special dish, like this classic seafood stew from Spain.

INGREDIENTS

1 cooked lobster
24 fresh mussels
1 large monkfish tail
15 ml / 1 tbsp plain flour
225 g / 8 oz squid rings
90 ml / 6 tbsp olive oil
12 large raw prawns

450 g / 1 lb ripe tomatoes
2 large mild onions
4 garlic cloves, crushed
30 ml / 2 tbsp brandy
2 bay leaves
5 ml / 1 tsp paprika
1 red chilli, seeded and chopped

300 ml / ½ pint / 1¼ cups fish stock
15 g / ½ oz / 3 tbsp ground almonds
30 ml / 2 tbsp chopped fresh parsley
salt and freshly ground black pepper

Serves 6

1

Cut the lobster in half and remove the dark intestine that runs down the length of the tail. Crack the claws using a hammer. Scrub the mussels, discarding any that are damaged and any open ones that do not close when tapped with a knife. Cut the monkfish fillets away from the central cartilage and cut each fillet into three.

2

Season the flour and toss the monkfish and squid in it. Heat the oil in a frying pan. Add the monkfish and squid and fry quickly; remove from the pan. Fry the prawns, then remove from the pan. Plunge the tomatoes into boiling water for 30 seconds, then refresh in cold water. Peel away the skins and chop roughly.

3

Chop the onions and add to the pan with two-thirds of the garlic. Fry for 3 minutes, then add the brandy and ignite with a taper. When the flames die down, add the tomatoes, bay leaves, paprika, chilli and stock. Bring to the boil, reduce the heat and simmer for 5 minutes.

4

Add the mussels, cover and cook for 3–4 minutes, until the shells have opened. Remove the mussels from the sauce and discard any that remain closed. Arrange all the fish, including the lobster, in a large flameproof serving dish.

5

Blend the ground almonds to a paste with the remaining garlic and parsley and stir into the sauce. Season with salt and pepper. Pour the sauce over the fish and lobster and cook gently for about 5 minutes until hot. Serve immediately with a green salad and plenty of warmed bread.

Poached Cod, Greek-style

Cod is often served with little preparation. Although it can be delicious in its simplest form, it sometimes deserves more sophisticated treatment. This recipe is a little more involved, poaching the fish with onions and tomatoes.

INGREDIENTS

300 ml / ½ pint / 1¼ cups olive oil
2 onions, thinly sliced
3 large well-flavoured tomatoes, roughly chopped
3 garlic cloves, thinly sliced
5 ml / 1 tsp granulated sugar
5 ml / 1 tsp chopped fresh dill
5 ml / 1 tsp chopped fresh mint
5 ml / 1 tsp chopped fresh celery leaves

15 ml / 1 tbsp chopped fresh parsley
300 ml / ½ pint / 1¼ cups water
6 cod steaks
juice of 1 lemon
salt and freshly ground black pepper
extra dill, mint or parsley, to garnish

Serves 6

1

Heat the oil in a large, shallow pan and cook the onions until pale golden. Stir in the tomatoes, garlic, sugar, dill, mint, celery leaves and parsley. Pour over the water. Season with salt and pepper, then simmer, uncovered, for 25 minutes, until the liquid has reduced by one-third.

2

Add the cod steaks and cook gently for 10–12 minutes, until the fish is just cooked. Remove from the heat and pour over the lemon juice. Cover and leave to stand for about 20 minutes before serving. Arrange the cod in a dish and spoon the sauce over the top. Garnish with herbs and serve warm or cold.

Stuffed Sardines

Adding a savoury sultana and pine nut stuffing takes sardines into a more sophisticated league.

8 fresh sardines
30 ml / 2 tbsp olive oil
75 g / 3 oz / 1½ cups breadcrumbs
50 g / 2 oz / ⅓ cup sultanas
50 g / 2 oz / ⅔ cup pine nuts
50 g / 2 oz can anchovy fillets, drained
60 ml / 4 tbsp chopped fresh parsley
1 onion, finely chopped
salt and freshly ground black pepper
lemon wedges, to garnish

Serves 4

3

Stuff each sardine with the mixture. Close the fish firmly and closely pack together in a single layer in an ovenproof dish.

4

Scatter any remaining filling over the sardines and drizzle with olive oil. Bake for 30 minutes and serve with lemon wedges.

1

Preheat the oven to 200°C / 400°F / Gas Mark 6. Gut and clean the sardines; dry with kitchen paper. Heat the oil in a frying pan and fry the breadcrumbs until golden.

2

Add the sultanas, pine nuts, anchovies, parsley, onion and seasoning to the breadcrumbs.

Seafood Risotto

Risotto is the perfect example of a rustic dish that can be adapted to take advantage of whatever is in season. This seafood version varies, depending on the current catch.

INGREDIENTS

60 ml / 4 tbsp sunflower oil
1 onion, chopped
2 garlic cloves, crushed
225 g / 8 oz / generous 1 cup arborio rice
105 ml / 7 tbsp white wine
1.5 litres / 2½ pints / 6 cups hot fish stock
350 g / 12 oz mixed seafood, such as raw prawns, mussels, squid rings or clams, prepared according to type
grated rind of ½ lemon
30 ml / 2 tbsp tomato purée
15 ml / 1 tbsp chopped fresh parsley
salt and freshly ground black pepper

Serves 4

1

Heat the oil in a heavy-based saucepan and fry the onion and garlic gently until soft. Add the rice and stir to coat the grains with oil. Pour in the wine and stir over a medium heat until it has been absorbed.

2

Ladle in 150 ml / ¼ pint / ⅔ cup of the hot stock and cook, stirring constantly, until the liquid is absorbed by the rice. Continue stirring and adding stock in similar quantities, until half is left. This should take about 10 minutes.

3

Stir in the seafood and cook for 2–3 minutes. Add the remaining stock as before, until the rice is cooked. It should be quite creamy and the grains just tender. Stir in the lemon rind, tomato purée and parsley. Season with salt and pepper and serve warm.

Italian Prawn Skewers

These are delicious, whether grilled or cooked on the barbecue, and would be ideal for a summer party.

INGREDIENTS

900 g / 2 lb raw tiger prawns, peeled
60 ml / 4 tbsp olive oil
45 ml / 3 tbsp vegetable oil
175 g / 6 oz / 1¼ cups very fine dry breadcrumbs
1 garlic clove, crushed
15 ml / 1 tbsp chopped fresh parsley
salt and freshly ground black pepper
lemon wedges, to serve

Serves 4

1

Slit the prawns down their backs and remove the dark veins. Rinse in cold water and pat dry. Mix the oils in a large bowl and add the prawns, turning them in the oil to coat evenly.

2

Add the breadcrumbs, garlic and parsley to the bowl, with salt and pepper to taste. Toss the oiled prawns in the mixture to coat them evenly. Cover and leave to marinate for 1 hour.

3

Preheat the grill. Thread the prawns on to four metal skewers, curling them up as you do so, so that the tail is skewered in the middle. Place the skewers in the grill pan and cook for about 2 minutes on each side, until the breadcrumbs are golden. Serve with lemon wedges.

POULTRY AND GAME

Turkey with Apples and Bay Leaves

*Apples from the orchard combine with bay leaves and Madeira to create
a delicious turkey casserole with a handsome garnish.*

INGREDIENTS

75 g / 3 oz / 6 tbsp butter
*675 g / 1½ lb turkey breast fillets,
cut into 2 cm / ¾ in slices*
4 tart cooking apples, peeled and sliced
3 bay leaves
90 ml / 6 tbsp Madeira
150 ml / ¼ pint / ⅔ cup chicken stock
10 ml / 2 tsp cornflour
150 ml / ¼ pint / ⅔ cup double cream
salt and freshly ground black pepper

Serves 4

1

Preheat the oven to 180°C / 350°F / Gas
Mark 4. Melt a third of the butter in a
large, shallow pan and fry the turkey breast
fillets until sealed on all sides. Transfer to a
casserole and add half the remaining butter
and half the apple slices and cook gently for
1–2 minutes.

2

Tuck the bay leaves around the turkey
breasts. Stir in 60 ml / 4 tbsp of the
Madeira and all the stock. Simmer for
3–4 minutes, then cover and bake for
40 minutes.

3

Mix the cornflour to a paste with a little of
the cream, then stir in the rest of the
cream. Add this mixture to the casserole,
season, stir well, then return to the oven for
10 minutes to allow the sauce to thicken.

4

To make the garnish, melt the remaining
butter in a frying pan and gently fry the
remaining apple slices until just tender.
Add the remaining Madeira and set it
alight. Once the flames have died down,
continue to cook the apple slices until they
are lightly browned. Arrange them on top
of the turkey mixture.

Chicken and Mushroom Cobbler

There's something very homely about a cobbler, with its scone topping and satisfying filling. Adding wild mushrooms enriches the flavour but button mushrooms are fine for a family meal.

INGREDIENTS

60 ml / 4 tbsp vegetable oil
1 onion, chopped
1 celery stick, sliced
1 small carrot, peeled and diced
3 skinless, boneless chicken breasts
450 g / 1 lb / 4 cups mixed field mushrooms and wild mushrooms, sliced
40 g / 1½ oz / 6 tbsp plain flour
500 ml / 18 fl oz / 2¼ cups hot chicken stock
10 ml / 2 tsp Dijon mustard
30 ml / 2 tbsp medium sherry
10 ml / 2 tsp wine vinegar
salt and freshly ground black pepper

For the cobbler topping
275 g / 10 oz / 2½ cups self-raising flour
pinch of celery salt
pinch of cayenne pepper
115 g / 4 oz / ½ cup butter, diced
50 g / 2 oz / ½ cup grated Cheddar cheese
150 ml / ¼ pint / ⅔ cup cold water
1 beaten egg, to glaze

Serves 4

1

Preheat the oven to 200°C / 400°F / Gas Mark 6. Heat the oil in a large, heavy-based saucepan and fry the onion, celery and carrot gently for 8–10 minutes, to soften without colouring. Cube the chicken, then add to the pan and cook briefly. Add the mushrooms, fry until the juices run, then stir in the flour.

2

Remove the pan from the heat and gradually stir in the stock. Return the pan to the heat, and simmer gently to thicken, stirring all the time. Stir in the mustard, sherry, vinegar and seasoning.

3

To make the topping, sift the flour, celery salt and cayenne into a bowl or food processor fitted with a metal blade. Rub in the butter and half the cheese until the mixture resembles coarse breadcrumbs. Add the water and combine without over-mixing.

4

Turn the dough on to a floured board, form it into a round and flatten to a thickness of about 1 cm / ½ in. Cut out as many 5 cm / 2 in shapes as you can, using a cutter.

5

Transfer the chicken mixture to a 1.2 litre / 2 pint / 5 cup pie dish, then overlap the cobbler shapes around the edge. Brush with beaten egg, scatter with the remaining cheese and bake for 25–30 minutes until the topping has risen well and is golden.

Roast Pheasant with Port

Many farmers – and their fortunate friends – have a regular supply of pheasant in the shooting season. This is an excellent way of cooking them.

INGREDIENTS

2 oven-ready hen pheasants, about
675 g / 1½ lb each
50 g / 2 oz / 4 tbsp butter, softened
8 fresh thyme sprigs
2 bay leaves
6 rindless streaky bacon rashers
15 ml / 1 tbsp plain flour
175 ml / 6 fl oz / ¾ cup game or
chicken stock, plus more if needed
15 ml / 1 tbsp redcurrant jelly
45–60 ml / 3–4 tbsp port
freshly ground black pepper

Serves 4

---1---

Preheat the oven to 230°C / 450°F / Gas Mark 8. Line a large roasting tin with a sheet of strong foil large enough to enclose the pheasants. Lightly brush the foil with oil.

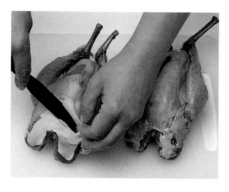

---2---

Wipe the pheasants with damp kitchen paper and remove any extra fat or skin. Using your fingertips, carefully loosen the skin of the breasts. Spread the butter between the skin and breast meat of each bird. Tie the legs securely with string, then lay the thyme sprigs and a bay leaf over the breast of each bird.

---3---

Lay the bacon over the breasts, place the birds in the foil-lined tin and season with pepper. Bring up the foil and enclose the birds. Roast for 20 minutes, then reduce the oven temperature to 190°C / 375°F / Gas Mark 5 and cook for 40 minutes more.

---4---

Uncover the birds and roast 10–15 minutes more. Transfer the birds to a board and leave to stand for 10 minutes before carving.

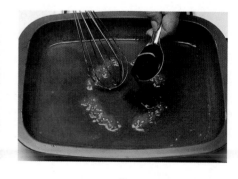

---5---

Pour the juices into the roasting tin and skim off any fat. Sprinkle in the flour and stir over a medium heat until smooth. Whisk in the stock and redcurrant jelly and bring to the boil. Simmer until the sauce thickens slightly, then stir in the port and adjust the seasoning. Strain and serve with the pheasants.

Duck Stew with Olives

In this traditional method of preparing duck the sweetness of the shallots balances the saltiness of the olives.

INGREDIENTS

*2 ducks, about 1.4 kg / 3¼ lb each,
quartered, or 8 duck leg quarters
225 g / 8 oz / 1½ cups shallots, peeled
30 ml / 2 tbsp plain flour
350 ml / 12 fl oz / 1½ cups dry red wine
475 ml / 16 fl oz / 2 cups duck or
chicken stock
1 bouquet garni
115 g / 4 oz / 1 cup stoned green or
black olives, or a combination
salt, if needed, and freshly ground
black pepper*

Serves 6–8

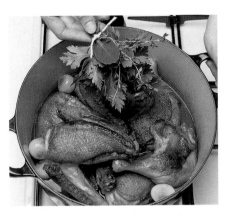

1

Put the duck portions, skin side down, in a large frying pan. Cook over a medium heat for 10–12 minutes until well browned, then turn to colour evenly. Cook in batches if necessary.

2

Pour 15 ml / 1 tbsp of the duck fat into a large, flameproof casserole. Place the casserole over a medium heat and cook the shallots until evenly browned, stirring frequently. Sprinkle with the flour and cook for 2 minutes more, stirring frequently.

3

Stir in the wine, then add the duck pieces, stock and bouquet garni. Bring to the boil, then reduce the heat, cover and simmer for about 40 minutes, stirring occasionally.

4

Rinse the olives in several changes of cold water. If they are very salty, put them in a saucepan, cover with water and bring to the boil, then drain and rinse. Add the stoned olives to the casserole and continue cooking for 20 minutes more, until the duck is very tender.

5

Transfer the duck pieces, shallots and olives to a plate. Strain the cooking liquid, skim off all the fat and return the liquid to the pan. Boil to reduce by about one-third, then adjust the seasoning and return the duck and vegetables to the casserole. Simmer gently for a few minutes to heat through and serve.

Pigeon Pie

This recipe is based upon a traditional dish, a filo pie filled with an unusual but delicious mixture of pigeon, eggs, spices and nuts. Chicken can be used instead of pigeon.

INGREDIENTS

3 pigeons
50 g / 2 oz / 4 tbsp butter
1 onion, chopped
1 cinnamon stick
½ tsp ground ginger
30 ml / 2 tbsp chopped fresh coriander
45 ml / 3 tbsp chopped fresh parsley
pinch of ground turmeric
15 ml / 1 tbsp caster sugar
¼ tsp ground cinnamon
115 g / 4 oz / 1 cup toasted almonds, finely chopped
6 eggs, beaten
salt and freshly ground black pepper
cinnamon and icing sugar, to garnish

For the pastry
175 g / 6 oz / ¾ cup butter, melted
16 sheets filo pastry
1 egg yolk

Serves 6

1

Wash the pigeons and place them in a heavy-based pan with the butter, onion, cinnamon stick, ginger, coriander, parsley and turmeric. Season with salt and pepper. Add just enough water to cover and bring to the boil. Reduce the heat, cover and simmer gently for about 1 hour, until the pigeon flesh is very tender.

2

Strain off the stock and reserve. Skin and bone the pigeons, and shred the flesh into bite-size pieces. Preheat the oven to 180°C / 350°F / Gas Mark 4. Mix the sugar, cinnamon and almonds in a bowl.

3

Measure 150 ml / ¼ pint / ⅔ cup of the reserved stock into a small pan. Add the eggs and mix well. Stir over a low heat until creamy and very thick and almost set. Season with salt and pepper.

4

Brush a 30 cm / 12 in diameter ovenproof dish with some of the melted butter and lay the first sheet of pastry in the dish. Brush this with butter and continue with five more sheets of pastry. Cover with the almond mixture, then half the egg mixture. Moisten with a little stock.

5

Layer four more sheets of filo pastry, brushing with butter as before. Lay the pigeon meat on top, then add the remaining egg mixture and more stock. Cover with all the remaining pastry, brushing each sheet with butter, and tuck in any overlap.

6

Brush the pie with egg yolk and bake for 40 minutes. Raise the oven temperature to 200°C / 400°F / Gas Mark 6, and bake for 15 minutes more, until the pastry is crisp and golden. Garnish with cinnamon and icing sugar in a lattice design. Serve hot.

Casseroled Rabbit with Thyme

This is the sort of home cooking found in farmhouse kitchens and cosy neighbourhood restaurants in France, where rabbit is treated much like chicken and enjoyed frequently.

INGREDIENTS

40 g / 1½ oz / 6 tbsp plain flour
1.2 kg / 2½ lb rabbit, cut into 8
portions
15 g / ½ oz / 1 tbsp butter
15 ml / 1 tbsp olive oil
250 ml / 8 fl oz / 1 cup red wine
350–475 ml / 12–16 fl oz / 1½–2
cups chicken stock
15 ml / 1 tbsp fresh thyme leaves
1 bay leaf
2 garlic cloves, finely chopped
10–15 ml / 2–3 tsp Dijon mustard
salt and freshly ground black pepper

Serves 4

1

Put the flour in a polythene bag and season with salt and pepper. One at a time, drop the rabbit pieces into the bag and shake to coat them with flour. Tap off the excess, then discard any remaining flour.

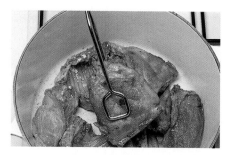

2

Melt the butter and oil in a flameproof casserole. Cook the rabbit pieces until golden.

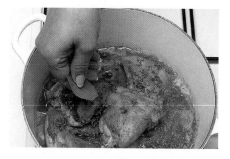

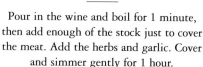

3

Pour in the wine and boil for 1 minute, then add enough of the stock just to cover the meat. Add the herbs and garlic. Cover and simmer gently for 1 hour.

4

Stir in the mustard. Lift the rabbit pieces on to a serving platter. Season the sauce, then strain it over the rabbit.

Farmhouse Venison Pie

This satisfying pie combines venison in a rich gravy with a potato and parsnip topping.

INGREDIENTS

45 ml / 3 tbsp sunflower oil
1 onion, chopped
1 garlic clove, crushed
3 rindless streaky bacon rashers,
chopped
675 g / 1½ lb minced venison
115 g / 4 oz / 1 cup button
mushrooms, chopped
30 ml / 2 tbsp plain flour
475 ml / 16 fl oz / 2 cups beef stock
150 ml / ¼ pint / ⅔ cup ruby port
2 bay leaves
5 ml / 1 tsp chopped fresh thyme
5 ml / 1 tsp Dijon mustard
15 ml / 1 tbsp redcurrant jelly
675 g / 1½ lb potatoes, peeled and cut
into large chunks
450 g / 1 lb parsnips, peeled and cut
into large chunks
1 egg yolk
50 g / 2 oz / 4 tbsp butter
grated nutmeg
45 ml / 3 tbsp chopped fresh parsley
salt and freshly ground black pepper

Serves 4

<u>2</u>

Meanwhile, preheat the oven to 200°C /
400°F / Gas Mark 6. Bring a saucepan of
lightly salted water to the boil and cook
the potatoes and parsnips for
20 minutes or until tender. Drain and
mash, then beat in the egg yolk, butter,
nutmeg and chopped parsley. Season to
taste with salt and pepper.

<u>3</u>

Spoon the venison mixture into a large pie
dish. Level the surface. Spread the potato
and parsnip mixture over the meat and
bake for 30–40 minutes, until piping hot
and golden brown. Serve at once.

<u>1</u>

Heat the oil in a large frying pan and fry
the onion, garlic and bacon for about
5 minutes. Add the venison and
mushrooms and cook for a few minutes,
stirring, until browned. Stir in the flour
and cook for 1–2 minutes, then add the
stock, port, herbs, mustard, redcurrant jelly
and seasoning. Bring to the boil, cover and
simmer for 30–40 minutes, until tender.

MEAT DISHES

 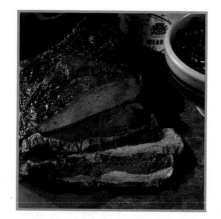 

Lamb with Mint and Lemon

Lamb has been served with mint for many years – it is a great combination.

INGREDIENTS

8 lamb steaks, 225 g/8 oz each
grated rind and juice of 1 lemon
2 cloves garlic, peeled and crushed
2 spring onions, finely chopped
2 tsp finely chopped fresh mint
leaves, plus some leaves for
garnishing
4 tbsp extra virgin olive oil
salt and black pepper

Serves 8

1

Make a marinade for the lamb by mixing all the other ingredients and seasoning to taste. Place the lamb steaks in a shallow dish and cover with the marinade. Refrigerate overnight.

2

Grill the lamb under a high heat until just cooked, basting with the marinade occasionally during cooking. Turn once during cooking. Serve garnished with fresh mint leaves.

Lamb and Leeks with Mint and Spring Onions

If you do not have any home-made chicken stock, use a good
quality ready-made stock rather than a stock cube.

INGREDIENTS

2 tbsp sunflower oil
2 kg/4 lb lamb (fillet or boned leg)
10 spring onions, thickly sliced
3 leeks, thickly sliced
1 tbsp flour
150 ml 1¼ pint white wine
300 ml 1½ pint chicken stock
1 tbsp tomato purée
1 tbsp sugar
salt and pepper
2 tbsp fresh mint leaves, finely
chopped, plus a few more to garnish
115 g/4 oz dried pears
1 kg/2 lb potatoes, peeled and sliced
30 g/1¼ oz melted butter

Serves 6

1

Heat the oil and fry the cubed lamb to seal it. Transfer to a casserole. Preheat the oven to 180°C/350°F/Gas Mark 4.

2

Fry the onions and leeks for 1 minute, stir in the flour and cook for another minute. Add the wine and stock and bring to the boil. Add the tomato purée, sugar, salt and pepper with the mint and chopped pears and pour into the casserole. Stir the mixture. Arrange the sliced potatoes on top and brush with the melted butter.

3

Cover and bake for 1½ hours. Then increase the temperature to 200°C/400°F/Gas Mark 6, cook for a further 30 minutes, uncovered, to brown the potatoes. Garnish with mint leaves.

Lamb Pie with Pear, Ginger and Mint Sauce

Cooking lamb with fruit is an idea taken from traditional Persian cuisine.

INGREDIENTS

1 boned mid-loin of lamb, 1 kg/2 lb
after boning
salt and pepper
8 large sheets filo pastry
25 g/1 oz/scant 2 tbsp butter

For the stuffing
1 tbsp butter
1 small onion, chopped
115 g/4 oz wholemeal breadcrumbs
grated rind of 1 lemon
170 g/6 oz drained canned pears from

a 400 g/14 oz can (rest
of can, and juice, used for sauce)
¼ tsp ground ginger
1 small egg, beaten
skewers, string and large needle to
make roll

For the sauce
rest of can of pears, including juice
2 tsp finely chopped fresh mint

Serves 6

1
Prepare the stuffing. Melt the butter in a pan and add the onion, cooking until soft. Preheat the oven to 180°C/350°F/Gas Mark 4. Put the butter and onion into a. mixing bowl and add the breadcrumbs, lemon rind, pears and ginger. Season lightly and add enough beaten egg to bind.

2
Spread the loin out flat, fat side down, and season. Place the stuffing along the middle of the loin and roll carefully, holding with skewers while you sew it together with string. Heat a large baking pan in the oven and brown the loin slowly on all sides. This will take 20–30 minutes. Leave to cool, and store in the refrigerator until needed.

3
Preheat the oven to 200°C/400°F/Gas Mark 6. Take two sheers of filo pastry and brush with melted butter. Overlap by about 13 cm/5 in to make a square. Place the next two sheets on top and brush with butter. Continue until all the pastry has been used.

4
Place the roll of lamb diagonally across one corner of the pastry, without overlapping the sides. Fold the corner over the lamb, fold in the sides, and brush the pastry well with melted butter. Roll to the far corner of the sheet. Place join side down on a buttered baking sheet and brush all over with the rest of the melted butter. Bake for about 30 minutes or until golden brown.

5
Blend the remaining pears with their juice and the mint, and serve with the lamb.

Pork and Black Bean Stew

This simple Spanish stew uses a few robust ingredients to create a deliciously intense flavour.

INGREDIENTS

275 g / 10 oz / 1½ cups black beans,
soaked overnight
675 g / 1½ lb boneless belly pork
rashers
60 ml / 4 tbsp olive oil
350 g / 12 oz baby onions or shallots
2 celery sticks, thickly sliced
10 ml / 2 tsp paprika
150 g / 5 oz chorizo sausage, chopped
600 ml / 1 pint / 2½ cups light
chicken or vegetable stock
2 green peppers, seeded and cut into
large pieces
salt and freshly ground pepper

Serves 5–6

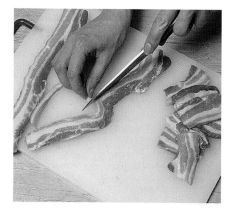

1

Preheat the oven to 160°C / 325°F / Gas
Mark 3. Drain the beans, place them in a
saucepan and cover with fresh water. Bring
to the boil, boil rapidly for 10 minutes,
then drain. Cut away any rind from the
pork and cut the meat into large chunks.

2

Heat the oil in a large frying pan and fry
the onions or shallots and celery for
3 minutes. Add the pork and fry for
5–10 minutes until the pork is browned.
Stir in the paprika and chorizo and fry for
2 minutes more. Transfer to an ovenproof
dish, add the beans and mix well.

3

Add the stock to the pan and bring to the
boil. Season lightly, then pour over the
meat and beans. Cover and bake for 1 hour,
then stir in the green peppers. Bake for
15 minutes more and serve hot.

NOTE
This is a good-natured stew which works
well with any winter vegetable. Try adding
chunks of leek, turnip, celeriac and even
little potatoes.

Pork and Sausage Casserole

This dish is based on a rural Spanish recipe. You should be able to find the butifarra sausages in a delicatessen but, if not, sweet Italian sausages will do.

INGREDIENTS

30 ml / 2 tbsp olive oil
4 boneless pork chops, about 175 g / 6 oz
4 butifarra or sweet Italian sausages
1 onion, chopped
2 garlic cloves, chopped
120 ml / 4 fl oz / ½ cup dry white wine
4 plum tomatoes, chopped
1 bay leaf
30 ml / 2 tbsp chopped fresh parsley
salt and freshly ground black pepper
green salad and baked potatoes, to serve

Serves 4

NOTE
Vine tomatoes, which are making a
welcome appearance in our supermarkets,
can be used instead of plum tomatoes.

1

Heat the oil in a large, deep frying pan.
Cook the pork chops over a high heat until
browned on both sides, then transfer
to a plate.

2

Add the sausages, onion and garlic to the
pan and cook over a moderate heat until
the sausages are browned and the onion
softened, turning the sausages two or three
times during cooking. Return the chops
to the pan.

3

Stir in the wine, tomatoes and bay leaf, and
season with salt and pepper. Add the
parsley. Cover the pan and cook for
30 minutes.

4

Remove the sausages from the pan and cut
into thick slices. Return them to the pan
and heat through. Serve hot, accompanied
by a green salad and baked potatoes.

Country Pie

*A classic raised pie. It takes quite a long time to make,
but is a perfect winter treat.*

1 small duck
1 small chicken
350 g/12 oz pork belly, minced
1 egg, lightly beaten
2 shallots, finely chopped
½ tsp ground cinnamon
½ tsp grated nutmeg
5 ml/1 tsp Worcestershire sauce
finely grated rind of 1 lemon
1/2 tsp freshly ground black pepper
150 ml/¼ pint/⅔ cup red wine
175 g/6 oz ham, cut into cubes
salt and freshly ground
black pepper

For the jelly
all the meat bones and trimmings
2 carrots
1 onion
2 celery sticks
15 ml/1 tbsp red wine
1 bay leaf
1 whole clove
1 sachet of gelatine
(about 15 g/1 oz)

For the pastry
225 g/8 oz/1 cup hard white fat
300 ml/½ pint/1¼ cups boiling
water
675 g/1½ lb/6 cups plain flour
1 egg, lightly beaten with a
pinch of salt

Serves 12

1

Cut as much meat from the raw duck and
chicken as possible, removing the skin and
sinews. Cut the duck and chicken breasts
into cubes and set them aside.

2

Mix the rest of the duck and chicken meat
with the minced pork, egg, shallots, spices,
Worcestershire sauce, lemon rind and salt
and pepper. Add the red wine and leave for
about 15 minutes for the flavours to develop.

3

To make the jelly, place the meat bones and
trimmings, carrots, onion, celery, wine, bay
leaf and clove in a large pan and cover with
2.75 litres/5 pints/12½ cups of water.
Bring to the boil, skimming off any scum,
and simmer gently for 2½ hours.

4

To make the pastry, place the fat and water
in a pan and bring to the boil. Sieve the flour
and a pinch of salt into a bowl and pour on
the liquid. Mix with a wooden spoon, and,
when the dough is cool enough to handle,
knead it well and let it sit in a warm place,
covered with a cloth, for 20–30 minutes or
until you are ready to use it. Preheat the
oven to 200°C/400°F/Gas Mark 6.

5

Grease a 25 cm/10 in loose-based deep cake tin. Roll out about two-thirds of the pastry thinly enough to line the cake tin. Make sure there are no holes and allow enough pastry to leave a little hanging over the top. Fill the pie with a layer of half the minced-pork mixture; then top this with a layer of the cubed duck and chicken breast-meat and cubes of ham. Top with the remaining minced pork. Brush the overhanging edges of pastry with water and cover with the remaining rolled-out pastry. Seal the edges well. Make two large holes in the top and decorate with any pastry trimmings.

6

Bake the pie for 30 minutes. Brush the top with the egg and salt mixture. Turn down the oven to 180°C/350°F/Gas Mark 4. After 30 minutes loosely cover the pie with foil to prevent the top getting too brown, and bake it for a further 1 hour.

7

Strain the stock after 2½ hours. Let it cool and remove the solidified layer of fat from the surface. Measure 600 ml/1 pint/2½ cups of stock. Heat it gently to just below boiling point and whisk the gelatine into it until no lumps are left. Add the remaining strained stock and leave to cool.

8

When the pie is cool, place a funnel through one of the holes and pour in as much of the stock as possible, letting it come up to the holes in the crust. Leave to set for at least 24 hours before slicing and serving.

Veal Kidneys with Mustard

This dish is equally delicious made with lamb's kidneys. Be sure not to cook the sauce too long after adding the mustard or it will lose its piquancy.

INGREDIENTS

*2 veal kidneys or 8–10 lamb's
kidneys, skinned
25 g / 1 oz / 2 tbsp butter
15 ml / 1 tbsp vegetable oil
115 g / 4 oz / 1 cup button
mushrooms, quartered
60 ml / 4 tbsp chicken stock
30 ml / 2 tbsp brandy (optional)
175 ml / 6 fl oz / ¾ cup crème fraîche
or double cream
30 ml / 2 tbsp Dijon mustard
salt and freshly ground black pepper
snipped fresh chives, to garnish*

Serves 4

___3___

Add the mushrooms to the pan and sauté
for 2–3 minutes until golden, stirring
frequently. Pour in the chicken stock and
brandy, if using, then bring to the boil and
boil for 2 minutes.

___4___

Stir in the cream and cook for about
2–3 minutes until the sauce is slightly
thickened. Stir in the mustard and seasoning,
then add the kidneys and cook for 1 minute.
Scatter over the chives before serving.

___1___

Cut the kidneys into pieces, discarding any
fat. If using lamb's kidneys, remove the
central core by cutting a V-shape from the
middle of each kidney. Cut each kidney
into three or four pieces.

___2___

Melt the butter with the oil in a large
frying pan. Add the kidneys, sauté over a
high heat for about 3–4 minutes, stirring
frequently, until well browned, then transfer
them to a plate using a slotted spoon.

Beef Rib with Onion Sauce

Beef with a peppercorn crust, seared in a pan and then briefly roasted in the oven, feeds two hungry farm workers or four people with less hearty appetites. The onion sauce is superb.

1 beef rib with bone, about 1 kg / 2¼ lb and about 4 cm / 1½ in thick, well trimmed of fat
5 ml / 1 tsp lightly crushed black peppercorns
15 ml / 1 tbsp coarse sea salt, crushed
50 g / 2 oz / 4 tbsp butter
1 large red onion, sliced
120 ml / 4 fl oz / ½ cup fruity red wine
120 ml / 4 fl oz / ½ cup beef stock
15–30 ml / 1–2 tbsp redcurrant jelly
¼ tsp dried thyme
30–45 ml / 2–3 tbsp olive oil
salt and freshly ground black pepper

Serves 2–4

1

Wipe the beef with damp kitchen paper. Mix the crushed peppercorns with the crushed salt and press the mixture on to both sides of the meat, coating it completely. Leave to stand, loosely covered, for 30 minutes.

2

Meanwhile, make the sauce. Melt 40 g / 1½ oz / 3 tbsp of the butter in a saucepan and cook the onion for 3–5 minutes until softened. Add the wine, stock, redcurrant jelly and thyme and bring to the boil. Reduce the heat and simmer for 30–35 minutes until the liquid has evaporated and the sauce has thickened. Season with salt and pepper and keep hot.

3

Preheat the oven to 220°C / 425°F / Gas Mark 7. Melt the remaining butter with the oil in a heavy, ovenproof frying pan. Add the meat and sear over a high heat for 1–2 minutes on each side. Immediately place the pan in the oven and roast for 8–10 minutes. Transfer the beef to a board, cover loosely and leave to stand for 10 minutes. With a knife, loosen the meat from the rib bone, then carve into thick slices. Serve with the onion sauce.

Roast Beef with Porcini and Roasted Sweet Peppers

A substantial and warming dish for cold, dark evenings.

INGREDIENTS

1.5 kg/3–3½ lb piece of sirloin
15 ml/1 tbsp olive oil
450 g/1 lb small red peppers
115 g/4 oz mushrooms
175 g/6 oz thick-sliced pancetta
or smoked bacon, cubed
50 g/2 oz/2 tbsp plain flour
150 ml/¼ pint/⅔ cup full-bodied
red wine
300 ml/½ pint/1¼ cups beef stock
30 ml/2 tbsp Marsala
10 ml/2 tsp dried mixed herbs
salt and freshly ground
black pepper

Serves 8

1

Preheat the oven to 190°C/375°F/
Gas Mark 5. Season the meat well. Heat the
olive oil in a large frying pan. When very
hot, brown the meat on all sides. Place in a
large roasting tin and cook for 1¼ hours.

2

Put the red peppers in the oven to roast for
20 minutes, if small ones are available, or
45 minutes if large ones are used.

3

Near the end of the meat's cooking time,
prepare the gravy. Roughly chop the
mushroom caps and stems.

4

Heat the frying pan again and add the
pancetta or bacon. Cook until the fat runs
freely from the meat. Add the flour and cook
for a few minutes until browned.

5

Gradually stir in the red wine and the stock.
Bring to the boil, stirring. Lower the heat
and add the Marsala, herbs and seasoning.

6

Add the mushrooms to the pan and heat
through. Remove the sirloin from the oven
and leave to stand for 10 minutes before
carving it. Serve with the roasted peppers
and the hot gravy.

DESSERTS

Lemon Meringue Bombe with Mint Chocolate

This easy ice cream will cause a sensation at a dinner party – it is unusual but quite the most delicious combination of tastes that you can imagine.

INGREDIENTS

2 large lemons
150 g/5 oz granulated sugar
3 small sprigs fresh mint
150 ml/¼ pint whipping cream
600 ml/1 pint natural yogurt
2 large meringues
225 g/8 oz good-quality mint chocolate, grated

Serves 6–8

1

Slice the rind off the lemons with a potato peeler, then squeeze them for juice. Place the lemon rind and sugar in a food processor and blend finely. Add the cream, yogurt and lemon juice and process thoroughly. Pour the mixture into a mixing bowl and add the meringues, roughly crushed.

3

When the ice cream has frozen, scoop out the middle and pour in the grated mint chocolate. Replace the ice cream to cover the chocolate and refreeze.

2

Reserve one of the mint sprigs and chop the rest finely. Add to the mixture. Pour into a 1.2 litre/2 pint glass bowl and freeze for 4 hours.

4

To turn out, dip the basin in very hot water for a few seconds to loosen the ice cream, then turn the basin upside down over the serving plate. Decorate with grated chocolate and a sprig of mint.

Mint Ice Cream

*This ice cream is best served slightly softened, so take it out of the freezer
20 minutes before you want to serve it. For a special occasion,
this looks spectacular served in an ice bowl.*

INGREDIENTS

*8 egg yolks
75 g/3 oz/6 tbsp caster sugar
600 ml/1 pint/2½ cups single
cream
1 vanilla pod
60 ml/4 tbsp chopped fresh mint*

Serves 8

1

Beat the egg yolks and sugar until they are
pale and light using a hand-held electric
beater or a balloon whisk. Transfer to a
small saucepan.

2

In a separate saucepan, bring the cream to
the boil with the vanilla pod.

3

Remove the vanilla pod and pour the hot
cream on to the egg mixture, whisking
briskly.

4

Continue whisking to ensure the eggs
are mixed into the cream.

5

Gently heat the mixture until the custard
thickens enough to coat the back of a
wooden spoon. Leave to cool.

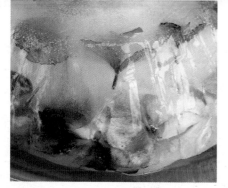

6

Stir in the mint and place in an ice-cream
maker to churn, about 3–4 hours. If you
don't have an ice-cream maker, freeze the
ice cream until mushy and then whisk it well
again, to break down the ice crystals. Freeze
for another 3 hours until it is softly frozen
and whisk again. Finally freeze until hard:
at least 6 hours.

Country Strawberry Fool

*Make this delicious fool on the day you want to eat it, and chill it well,
for the best strawberry taste.*

300 ml/½ pint/1¼ cups milk
2 egg yolks
90 g/3½ oz/scant ½ cup
caster sugar
few drops of vanilla essence
900 g/2 lb ripe strawberries
juice of ½ lemon
300 ml/½ pint/1¼ cups double
cream

To decorate
12 small strawberries
4 fresh mint sprigs

Serves 4

1

First make the custard. Whisk 30 ml/2 tbsp
milk with the egg yolks, 15 ml/1 tbsp caster
sugar and the vanilla essence.

2

Heat the remaining milk until it is just
below boiling point.

3

Stir the milk into the egg mixture. Rinse
the pan out and return the mixture to it.

4

Gently heat and whisk until the mixture
thickens (it should be thick enough to coat
the back of a spoon). Lay a wet piece of
greaseproof paper on top of the custard and
leave it to cool.

5

Purée the strawberries in a food processor or
blender with the lemon juice and the
remaining sugar.

6

Lightly whip the cream and fold in the fruit
purée and custard. Pour into glass dishes and
decorate with the whole strawberries and
sprigs of mint.

Mixed Berry Tart

The orange-flavoured pastry is delicious with the fresh fruits of summer.
Serve this with some extra shreds of orange rind scattered on top.

INGREDIENTS

For the pastry
225 g/8 oz/2 cups plain flour
115 g/4 oz/½ cup unsalted
butter
finely grated rind of 1 orange,
plus extra to decorate

For the filing
300 ml/½ pint/1¼ cups
crème fraîche
finely grated rind of 1 lemon
10 ml/2 tsp icing sugar
675 g/1½ lb mixed
summer berries

Serves 8

1

To make the pastry, put the flour and butter
in a large bowl. Rub in the butter until the
mixture resembles breadcrumbs.

2

Add the orange rind and enough cold water
to make a soft dough.

3

Roll into a ball and chill for at least
30 minutes. Roll out the pastry on a
lightly floured surface.

4

Line a 23 cm/9 in loose-based flan tin with
the pastry. Chill for 30 minutes. Preheat the
oven to 200°C/400°F/Gas Mark 6 and
place a baking sheet in the oven to heat up.
Line the tin with greaseproof paper and
baking beans and bake blind on the baking
sheet for 15 minutes. Remove the paper
and beans and bake for 10 minutes more,
until the pastry is golden. Allow to
cool completely. To make the filling,
whisk the crème fraîche, lemon rind and
sugar together and pour into the pastry case
Top with fruit, sprinkle with orange
rind and serve sliced.

Lemon Meringue Pie

This tasty pie would make a perfect end to a simple summer picnic. Served cold, it needs no accompaniment.

grated rind and juice of 1 large lemon
250 ml / 8 fl oz / 1 cup water
25 g / 1 oz / 2 tbsp butter
200 g / 7 oz / scant 1 cup sugar
45 ml / 3 tbsp cornflour mixed to a
paste with 15 ml / 1 tbsp water
3 eggs, separated
pinch each of salt and cream of tartar

For the pastry
115 g / 4 oz / 1 cup plain flour
½ tsp salt
75 g / 3 oz / 6 tbsp hard white
vegetable fat, diced
30 ml / 2 tbsp iced water

Serves 8

NOTE
For Lime Meringue Pie, substitute the grated rind and juice of 2 medium-size limes for the lemon.

1

For the pastry, sift the flour and salt into a bowl. Rub in the fat until the mixture resembles breadcrumbs. Stir in just enough water to bind the dough and roll out.

2

Line a 23 cm / 9 in flan tin with the pastry, allowing the pastry to overhang the edge by 1 cm / ½ in. Fold the overhang under and crimp the edges. Chill the pastry case for at least 20 minutes. Preheat the oven to 200°C / 400°F / Gas Mark 6.

3

Prick the pastry all over with a fork. Line with crumpled foil and bake for 12 minutes. Remove the foil and bake for 6–8 minutes more, until golden.

4

In a saucepan, combine the lemon rind and juice with the water. Add the butter and 115g / 4 oz / ½ cup of the sugar. Bring the mixture to the boil. Mix the cornflour paste with the egg yolks. Add to the lemon mixture and return to the boil, whisking continuously for about 5 minutes until the mixture thickens. Cover the surface with damp, greaseproof paper to prevent a skin from forming. Leave to cool.

5

For the meringue, beat the egg whites with the salt and cream of tartar until they hold stiff peaks. Add the remaining sugar and beat until glossy.

6

Spoon the lemon mixture into the pastry case and spread level. Spoon the meringue on top, smoothing it up to the edge of the pastry to seal. Bake for 12–15 minutes, or until the meringue is tinged with gold.

Orange-blossom Jelly

A fresh orange jelly makes a delightful dessert: the natural fruit flavour combined with the smooth jelly has a cleansing quality that is especially welcome after a rich main course. This is delicious served with thin, crisp langues de chat biscuits.

INGREDIENTS

65 g/2½ oz/5 tbsp caster sugar
150 ml/¼ pint ⅔ cup water
2 sachets of gelatine
(about 25 g/1 oz)
600 ml/1 pint/2½ cups freshly
squeezed orange juice
30 ml/2 tbsp orange-flower water

Serves 4–6

1

Place the caster sugar and water in a small saucepan and gently heat to dissolve the sugar. Leave to cool.

2

Sprinkle over the gelatine, ensuring it is completely submerged in the water. Leave to stand until the gelatine has absorbed all the liquid and is solid.

3

Gently melt the gelatine over a bowl of simmering water until it becomes clear and transparent. Leave to cool. When the gelatine is cold, mix it with the orange juice and orange-flower water.

4

Wet a jelly mould and pour in the jelly. Chill in the refrigerator for at least 2 hours, or until set. Turn out to serve.

Steamed Ginger and Cinnamon Syrup Pudding

A traditional and comforting steamed pudding, best served with custard.

120 g/4½ oz/9 tbsp softened
butter
45 ml/3 tbsp golden syrup
115 g/4 oz/½ cup caster sugar
2 eggs, lightly beaten
115 g/4 oz/1 cup plain flour
5 ml/1 tsp baking powder
5 ml/1 tsp ground cinnamon
25 g/1 oz stem ginger,
finely chopped
30 ml/2 tbsp milk

Serves 4

1

Set a full steamer or saucepan of water on to boil. Lightly grease a 600 ml/1 pint/2½ cup pudding basin with 15 g/½ oz/1 tbsp butter. Place the golden syrup in the basin.

2

Cream the remaining butter and sugar together until light and fluffy. Gradually add the eggs until the mixture is glossy. Sift the flour, baking powder and cinnamon together and fold them into the mixture, with the stem ginger. Add the milk to make a soft, dropping consistency.

3

Spoon the batter into the basin and smooth the top. Cover with a pleated piece of greaseproof paper, to allow for expansion during cooking. Tie securely with string and steam for 1½–2 hours, making sure that the water level is kept topped up, to ensure a good flow of steam to cook the pudding. Turn the pudding out to serve it.

Poached Pears

Serve warm with clotted cream and crisp shortbread fingers.

INGREDIENTS

6 medium pears
350 g/12 oz/1¾ cups caster sugar
75 ml/5 tbsp runny honey
1 vanilla pod
600 ml/1 pint/2½ cups red wine
5 ml/1 tsp whole cloves
7 cm/3 in cinnamon stick

Serves 4

1

Peel the pears but leave them whole, keeping the stalks as well.

2

Put the sugar, honey, vanilla pod, wine, cloves and cinnamon stick in a large pan.

3

Add the pears and poach until soft, about 30 minutes. When the pears are tender, remove them with a slotted spoon and keep them warm. Remove the vanilla pod, cloves and cinnamon stick and boil the liquid until it is reduced by half. Serve spooned over the pears.

Cherry Clafoutis

This is a traditional French Farmhouse way of serving fresh cherries.

INGREDIENTS

675 g / 1½ lb / 6 cups fresh cherries
50 g / 2oz / ½ cup plain flour
pinch of salt
4 eggs, plus 2 egg yolks
115 g / 4oz / ½ cup caster sugar, plus
extra for dusting
600 ml / 1 pint / 2½ cups milk
50 g / 2 oz / ¼ cup melted butter, plus
extra for greasing

Serves 6

1

Preheat the oven to 190°C / 375°F / Gas Mark 5. Lightly butter the base and sides of a shallow ovenproof dish. Stone the cherries and place them in a single layer in the dish.

2

Sift the flour and salt into a bowl. Add the eggs, egg yolks, sugar and a little of the milk and whisk to a smooth batter.

3

Gradually whisk in the rest of the milk and the melted butter, then strain the batter over the cherries. Bake for 40–50 minutes until golden and just set. Serve warm, dusted with caster sugar.

NOTE

If fresh cherries are not available use two 425 g / 15 oz cans stoned black cherries, thoroughly drained. For a special dessert, add 45 ml / 3 tbsp Kirsch or cherry brandy to the batter.

Blackberry Charlotte

A classic pudding, perfect for cold days. Serve with lightly whipped cream or home-made custard.

INGREDIENTS

65 g/2½ oz/5 tbsp unsalted butter
175 g/6 oz/3 cups fresh white breadcrumbs
50 g/2 oz/4 tbsp soft brown sugar
60 ml/4 tbsp golden syrup
finely grated rind and juice of 2 lemons
50 g/2 oz walnut halves
450 g/1 lb blackberries
450 g/1 lb cooking apples, peeled, cored and finely sliced

Serves 4

1

Preheat the oven to 180°C/350°F/ Gas Mark 4. Grease a 450 ml/¾ pint/ 2 cup dish with 15 g/½ oz/1 tbsp of the butter. Melt the remaining butter and add the breadcrumbs. Sauté them for 5–7 minutes, until the crumbs are a little crisp and golden. Leave to cool slightly.

2

Place the sugar, syrup, lemon rind and juice in a small saucepan and gently warm them. Add the crumbs.

3

Process the walnuts until they are finely ground.

4

Arrange a thin layer of blackberries on the dish. Top with a thin layer of crumbs.

5

Add a thin layer of apple, topping it with another thin layer of crumbs. Repeat the process with another layer of blackberries, followed by a layer of crumbs. Continue until you have used up all the ingredients, finishing with a layer of crumbs.

The mixture should be piled well above the top edge of the dish, because it shrinks during cooking. Bake for 30 minutes, until the crumbs are golden and the fruit is soft.

BREADS, BAKES
AND CAKES

Wholemeal Bread

Home-made bread creates one of the most evocative smells in country cooking.
Eat this on the day of making, to enjoy the superb fresh taste.

INGREDIENTS

20 g/³⁄₄ oz fresh yeast
300 ml/¹⁄₂ pint/1¹⁄₄ cups
lukewarm milk
5 ml/1 tsp caster sugar
225 g/8 oz/1¹⁄₂ cups strong
wholemeal flour, sifted
225 g/8 oz/2 cups strong
white flour, sifted
5 ml/1 tsp salt
50 g/2 oz/4 tbsp butter,
chilled and cubed
1 egg, lightly beaten
30 ml/2 tbsp mixed seeds

Makes 4 rounds or 2 loaves

1

Gently dissolve the yeast with a little of the milk and the sugar to make a paste. Place both the flours plus any bran from the sieve and the salt in a large warmed mixing bowl. Rub in the butter until the mixture resembles breadcrumbs.

2

Add the yeast mixture, remaining milk and egg and mix into a fairly soft dough. Knead on a floured board for 15 minutes. Lightly grease the mixing bowl and put the dough back in the bowl, covering it with a piece of greased cling film. Leave to double in size in a warm place (this should take at least an hour).

3

Knock the dough back and knead it for a further 10 minutes. Preheat the oven to 200°C/400°F/Gas Mark 6. To make round loaves, divide the dough into four pieces and shape them into flattish rounds. Place them on a floured baking sheet and leave to rise for a further 15 minutes. Sprinkle the loaves with the mixed seeds. Bake for about 20 minutes until golden and firm.

NOTE

For tin-shaped loaves, put the knocked-back dough into two greased loaf tins instead. Leave to rise for a further 45 minutes and then bake for about 45 minutes, until the loaf sounds hollow when turned out of the tin and knocked on the base.

Olive Bread

Olive breads are popular all over the Mediterranean. For this Greek recipe use rich, oily olives or those marinated in herbs rather than canned ones.

INGREDIENTS

2 red onions
30 ml / 2 tbsp olive oil
225 g / 8 oz / 1⅓ cups pitted black or green olives
800 g / 1¾ lb / 7 cups strong white flour
7.5 ml / 1½ tsp salt
20 ml / 4 tsp easy-blend dried yeast
45 ml / 3 tbsp roughly chopped fresh parsley, coriander or mint
475 ml / 16 fl oz / 2 cups hand-hot water

Makes 2 x 675g / 1½ lb loaves

VARIATION
Shape the dough into 16 small rolls. Slash the tops as below and reduce the cooking time to 25 minutes.

1
Slice the onions thinly. Fry them gently in the oil until soft. Roughly chop the olives.

2
Put the flour, salt, yeast and parsley, coriander or mint in a large bowl. Stir in the olives and fried onions, then pour in the hand-hot water. Mix to a dough, adding a little more water if the mixture feels dry.

3
Knead on a lightly floured surface for about 10 minutes, until smooth and elastic. Cut the dough in half. Shape into two rounds and place on two oiled baking sheets. Cover loosely with lightly oiled clear film and leave until doubled in size.

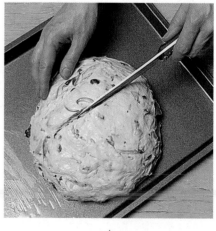

4
Preheat the oven to 220°C / 425°F / Gas Mark 7. Slash the tops of the loaves with a knife. Bake for about 40 minutes or until the loaves sound hollow when tapped on the bottom. Transfer to a wire rack to cool.

Easter Plait

Serve this delicious plait sliced with butter and jam.
It is also very good toasted on the day after you made it.

INGREDIENTS

200 ml/7 floz/⁷⁄₈ cup milk
2 eggs, lightly beaten
450 g/1 lb/4 cups plain flour
½ tsp salt
10 ml/2 tsp ground mixed spice
75 g/3 oz/6 tbsp butter
20 g/¾ oz dried yeast
75 g/3 oz/6 tbsp caster sugar
175 g/6oz/1¼ cups currants

25 g/1 oz/¼ cup candied mixed
peel, chopped
a little sweetened milk, to glaze
25 g/1 oz/1½ tbsp glacé
cherries, chopped
15 g/½ oz/1 tbsp angelica,
chopped

Serves 8

1

Warm the milk to lukewarm, add two-thirds of it to the eggs and mix well.

2

Sift the flour, salt and mixed spice together. Rub in the butter, then add the sugar and dried yeast. Make a well in the centre, and add the milk mixture, adding more milk as necessary to make a sticky dough.

3

Knead on a well-floured surface and then knead in the currants and mixed peel, reserving 15 ml/1 tbsp for the topping. Put the dough in a lightly greased bowl and cover it with a damp tea towel. Leave to double its size. Preheat the oven to 220°C/425°F/Gas Mark 7.

4

Turn the dough out on to a floured surface and knead again for 2–3 minutes. Divide the dough into three even pieces. Roll each piece into a sausage shape roughly 20 cm/8 in long. Plait the three pieces together, turning under and pinching each end. Place on a floured baking sheet and leave to rise for 15 minutes.

5

Brush the top with sweetened milk and scatter with roughly chopped cherries, strips of angelica and the reserved mixed peel. Bake in the preheated oven for 45 minutes or until the bread sounds hollow when tapped on the bottom. Cool slightly on a wire rack.

Scones

The secret with making scones is not to overwork the dough.

INGREDIENTS

225 g / 8 oz / 2 cups plain flour
5 ml / 1 tsp baking powder
½ tsp bicarbonate of soda
5 ml / 1 tsp salt
50 g / 2 oz / ¼ cup butter or
margarine, chilled
175 ml / 6 fl oz / ¾ cup buttermilk or
soured milk

Makes 10

1

Preheat the oven to 220°C / 425°F / Gas Mark 7. Sift the dry ingredients into a mixing bowl. Mix in the butter or margarine with a fork until the mixture resembles coarse breadcrumbs.

2

Add the buttermilk or soured milk and mix swiftly to a soft dough.

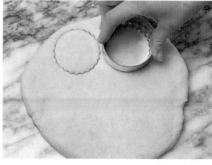

3

Knead the dough on a lightly floured board for 30 seconds.

4

Roll or pat out the dough to a thickness of 1 cm / ½ in. Use a floured 6 cm / 2½ in pastry cutter to cut out 10 rounds. Transfer the rounds to a baking sheet and bake for 10–12 minutes, until well risen and golden brown.

Butter Biscuits

These little biscuits are similar to shortbread, but richer.
Handle them with care, as they break easily.

INGREDIENTS

200 g / 7 oz / ¾ cup butter, diced,
plus extra for greasing
6 egg yolks, lightly beaten
15 ml / 1 tbsp milk
225 g / 8 oz / 2 cups plain flour
175 g / 6 oz / ¾ cup caster sugar

Makes 18–20

1

Preheat the oven to 180°C / 350°F / Gas Mark 4. Lightly butter a large, heavy baking sheet. Mix 15 ml / 1 tbsp of the beaten egg yolks with the milk, to make a glaze, and set aside.

2

Sift the flour into a large bowl and make a well in the centre. Add the remaining egg yolks, sugar and butter and, using your fingertips, work them together until smooth and creamy.

3

Gradually incorporate the flour to make a smooth, slightly sticky dough.

4

Using floured hands, pat out the dough to a thickness of 8 mm / ⅜ in and cut out rounds using a 7.5 cm / 3 in cutter. Transfer the rounds to a baking sheet, brush each with a little egg glaze, then using the back of a knife, score to create a lattice pattern.

5

Bake for 12–15 minutes until golden. Cool in the tin on a wire rack for 15 minutes, then carefully remove the biscuits and leave to cool completely on the rack.

Orange Shortbread Fingers

These are a real tea-time treat. The fingers will keep in an airtight tin for up to two weeks.

INGREDIENTS

115 g/4 oz/½ cup unsalted butter, softened
50 g/2 oz/4 tbsp caster sugar, plus a little extra
finely grated rind of 2 oranges
175 g/6 oz/1½ cups plain flour

Makes 18

1

Preheat the oven to 190°C/375°F/ Gas Mark 5. Beat the butter and sugar together until they are soft and creamy. Beat in the orange rind.

2

Gradually add the flour and gently pull the dough together to form a soft ball. Roll the dough out on a lightly floured surface until about 1 cm/½ in thick. Cut it into fingers, sprinkle over a little extra caster sugar, prick with a fork and bake for about 20 minutes, or until the fingers are a light golden colour.

Pound Cake

This orange-scented cake is good for tea or as a dessert with a fruit sauce.

INGREDIENTS

*450 g / 1 lb / 3 cups fresh raspberries,
strawberries or stoned cherries, or a
combination of any of these
225 g / 8 oz / 1 cup caster sugar, plus
extra for sprinkling
15 ml / 1 tbsp lemon juice
175 g / 6 oz / 1½ cups plain flour
10 ml / 2 tsp baking powder
pinch of salt
175 g / 6 oz / ¾ cup butter, softened
3 eggs
grated rind of 1 orange
15 ml / 1 tbsp orange juice*

Serves 6–8

1

Reserve a few whole fruits for decorating. In a food processor fitted with the metal blade, process the remaining fruit until smooth. Add 30 ml / 2 tbsp of the sugar and the lemon juice, then process again to combine. Strain the sauce and chill.

2

Base-line and grease a 20 x 10 cm / 8 x 4 in loaf tin. Sprinkle the base and sides of the tin lightly with sugar and tip out any excess. Preheat the oven to 180°C / 350°F / Gas Mark 4.

3

Sift the flour with the baking powder and salt. In a medium bowl, beat the butter until creamy. Add the remaining sugar and beat for 4–5 minutes until very light and fluffy, then add the eggs, one at a time, beating well after each addition. Beat in the orange rind and juice.

4

Gently fold in the flour mixture in batches, then spoon the mixture into the prepared tin and tap gently to release any air bubbles. Bake for 35–40 minutes until the top of the cake is golden and springs back when touched. Cool in the tin for 10 minutes, then transfer the cake to a wire rack and cool for 30 minutes more. Remove the lining paper and serve slices or wedges of the warm cake with a little of the fruit sauce. Decorate with the reserved fruit.

Light Fruit Cake

This is not the conventional fruit cake mixture, but it is moist, rich and absolutely delicious.

INGREDIENTS

225 g / 8 oz / 1⅓ cups ready-to-eat
prunes
225 g / 8 oz / 1⅓ cups dates
225 g / 8 oz / 1⅓ cups currants
225 g / 8 oz / 1⅓ cups sultanas
250 ml / 8 fl oz / 1 cup dry white wine
250 ml / 8 fl oz / 1 cup rum
350 g / 12 oz / 3 cups plain flour
10 ml / 2 tsp baking powder
5 ml / 1 tsp ground cinnamon
½ tsp grated nutmeg
225 g / 8 oz / 1 cup butter, at room
temperature
225 g / 8 oz / 1 cup granulated sugar
4 eggs, lightly beaten
5 ml / 1 tsp vanilla essence

Makes 2 loaves

1

Pit the prunes and dates and chop finely.
Place in a bowl with the currants and
sultanas. Stir in the wine and rum. Cover
and leave to stand for 48 hours. Stir
occasionally.

2

Preheat the oven to 150°C / 300°F / Gas
Mark 2. Line and grease two 23 x 13 cm /
9 x 5 in loaf tins. Sift the flour, baking
powder, cinnamon and nutmeg into a bowl.

3

Cream the butter and sugar together until
light and fluffy. Gradually add the eggs and
vanilla essence. Fold in the flour mixture in
batches, then add the dried fruit mixture
and its liquid. Mix lightly.

4

Divide the mixture between the tins and
bake for about 1½ hours, or until a skewer
inserted in a loaf comes out clean. Cool in
the tin for 20 minutes, then transfer to a
wire rack to cool completely.

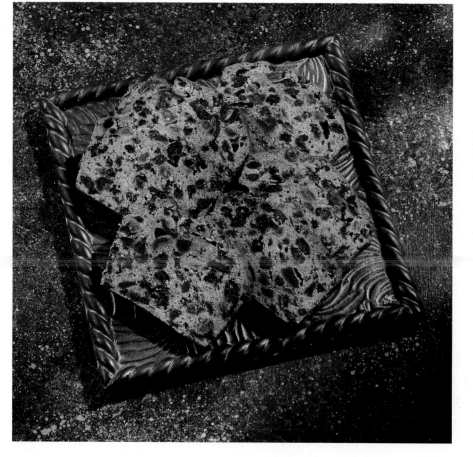

Lemon Drizzle Cake

You can also make this recipe using a large orange instead of the lemons; either way, it makes a zesty treat for afternoon tea.

INGREDIENTS

finely grated rind of 2 lemons
175 g/6 oz/12 tbsp caster sugar
*225 g/8 oz/1 cup unsalted
butter, softened*
4 eggs
*225 g/8 oz/2 cups self-raising
flour*
5 ml/1 tsp baking powder
¼ tsp salt
*shredded rind of 1 lemon,
to decorate*

For the syrup
juice of 1 lemon
150 g/5 oz/¾ cup caster sugar

Serves 6

1

Preheat the oven to 160°C/325°F/
Gas Mark 3. Grease a 1 kg/2 lb loaf tin or
18–20 cm/7–8 in round cake tin and line it
with greaseproof paper or baking parchment.
Mix the lemon rind and caster sugar together.

2

Cream the butter with the lemon and sugar
mixture. Add the eggs and mix until
smooth. Sift the flour, baking powder and
salt into a bowl and fold a third at a time into
the mixture. Turn the batter into the tin,
smooth the top and bake for 1½ hours or
until golden brown and springy to the touch.

3

To make the syrup, slowly heat the juice
with the sugar and dissolve it gently. Make
several slashes in the top of the cake and pour
over the syrup. Sprinkle the shredded lemon
rind and 5 ml/1 tsp granulated sugar on top
and leave to cool.

PICKLES AND PRESERVES

Spiced Pickled Pears

*These delicious pears are the perfect accompaniment for cooked ham
or cold meat salads.*

900 g/2 lb pears
600 ml/1 pint/2½ cups
white-wine vinegar
225 g/8 oz/1⅛ cups caster sugar
1 cinnamon stick
5 star anise
10 whole cloves

Makes 900 g/2 lb

1

Peel the pears, keeping them whole
and leaving on the stalks. Heat the vinegar
and sugar together until the sugar has melted.
Pour over the pears and poach for 15 minutes.

2

Add the cinnamon, star anise and cloves
and simmer for 10 minutes. Remove the
pears and pack tightly into sterilized jars.
Simmer the syrup for a further 15 minutes
and pour it over the pears. Seal the jars
tightly and store in a cool, dark place. The
pears will keep for up to a year unopened.
Once opened, store in the fridge and
consume within a week.

Piccalilli

The piquancy of this relish partners well with sausages, bacon or ham.

INGREDIENTS

675 g/1½ lb cauliflower
450 g/1 lb small onions
350 g/12 oz French beans
5 ml/1 tsp ground turmeric

5 ml/1 tsp dry mustard powder
10 ml/2 tsp cornflour
600 ml/1 pint/2½ cups vinegar

Makes 3 × 450 g/1 lb jars

1

Cut the cauliflower into tiny florets.

2

Peel the onions and top and tail
the French beans.

3

In a small saucepan, measure in the turmeric,
mustard powder and cornflour, and pour
over the vinegar. Stir well and simmer
for 10 minutes.

4

Pour the vinegar mixture over the vegetables
in a pan, mix well and simmer
for 45 minutes.

5

Pour into sterilized jars. Seal each jar with a
waxed disc and a tightly fitting cellophane
top. Store in a cool dark place. The piccalilli
will keep unopened for up to a year. Once
opened store in the fridge and consume
within a week.

Mint Sauce

Mint sauce is the classic accompaniment to roast lamb.

INGREDIENTS

1 large bunch mint
105 ml / 7 tbsp boiling water
150 ml / ¼ pint / ⅔ cup wine vinegar
30 ml / 2 tbsp granulated sugar

Makes 250 ml / 8 fl oz / 1 cup

1

Chop the mint finely and place it in a 600 ml / 1 pint / 2½ cup jug. Pour on the boiling water and leave to infuse. When lukewarm, add the vinegar and sugar. Pour into a clean bottle and store in the fridge.

Tomato Ketchup

The true tomato taste shines through in this homemade sauce.

INGREDIENTS

2.25 kg / 5–5¼ lb very ripe tomatoes
1 onion
6 cloves
4 allspice berries
6 black peppercorns
1 fresh rosemary sprig
25 g / 1 oz fresh root ginger, sliced
1 celery heart, chopped
30 ml / 2 tbsp soft brown sugar
60 ml / 4 tbsp raspberry vinegar
3 garlic cloves, peeled
15 ml / 1 tbsp salt

Makes 2.75 kg / 6 lb

1

Skin and seed the tomatoes, then chop them finely and place in a large saucepan. Stud the onion with the cloves, tie it with the allspice, peppercorns, rosemary and ginger in a double layer of muslin and add to the saucepan. Stir in the celery, sugar, vinegar, garlic and salt.

2

Bring the mixture to the boil over a high heat, stirring occasionally. Reduce the heat and simmer for 1½–2 hours, stirring frequently until reduced by half. Purée the mixture in a blender or food processor, then return to the pan and bring to the boil. Reduce the heat and simmer for 15 minutes, then bottle in clean, sterilized jars. Store in the fridge. Use within 2 weeks.

Traditional Horseradish Sauce

Fresh horseradish root is extremely potent, but its effects can be alleviated if it is scrubbed and peeled underwater and a food processor is used to do the fine chopping or grating.

INGREDIENTS

45 ml / 3 tbsp horseradish root, freshly grated
15 ml / 1 tbsp white wine vinegar
5 ml / 1 tsp caster sugar
pinch of salt
150 ml / ¼ pint / ⅔ cup thick double cream, for serving

Makes about 175 ml / 6 fl oz / ¾ cup

1

Place the grated horseradish in a bowl. Stir in the vinegar, sugar and a pinch of salt.

2

Pour the sauce into a sterilized jar. It can be kept for up to 6 months in the fridge. A couple of hours before you intend to serve it, stir in the cream.

OPPOSITE: *Each of these sauces is a powerful reduction of its main ingredients.*

Strawberry Jam

This classic recipe is always popular. Make sure the jam is allowed to cool before pouring into jars so the fruit doesn't float to the top.

INGREDIENTS

1.5 kg/3–3½ lb strawberries
juice of ½ lemon
1.5 kg/3–3½ lb granulated sugar

Makes about 2.25 kg/5 lb

1

Hull the strawberries.

2

Put the strawberries in a pan with the lemon juice. Mash a few of the strawberries. Let the fruit simmer for 20 minutes or until softened.

3

Add the sugar and let it dissolve slowly over a gentle heat. Then let the jam boil rapidly until a setting point is reached.

4

Leave to stand until the strawberries are well distributed through the jam. Pot into sterilized jars. Seal each jar with a waxed disc and cover with a tightly fitting cellophane top. Store in a cool dark place. The jam may be kept unopened for up to a year. Once opened, keep in the fridge and consume within a week.

Three-fruit Marmalade

Home-made marmalade may be time-consuming but the results are incomparably better than store-bought varieties.

INGREDIENTS

350 g/12 oz oranges
350 g/12 oz lemons
700 g/1 ½ lb grapefruit
2.5 litres/4½ pints/10¼ cups water
2.75 kg/6 lb granulated sugar

Makes 6 × 450 g/1 lb jars

1

Rinse and dry the fruit.

2

Put the fruit in a preserving pan. Add the water and let it simmer for about 2 hours.

3

Quarter the fruit, remove the pulp and add it to the pan with the cooking liquid.

4

Cut the rinds into slivers, and add to the pan. Add the sugar. Gently heat until the sugar has dissolved. Bring to the boil and cook until a setting point is reached. Leave to stand for 1 hour to allow the peel to settle. Pour into sterilized jars. Seal each jar with a waxed disc and a tightly fitting cellophane top. Store in a cool, dark place.

Index